King Vultures

By Jim Redmond

Raintree
A Division of Reed Elsevier, Inc.
Chicago, Illinois
www.raintreelibrary.com

ANIMALS OF THE RAIN FOREST

For information, address the publisher:
Raintree, 100 N. LaSalle, Suite 1200, Chicago, IL 60602

Library of Congress Cataloging-in-Publication Data
Redmond, Jim.
  King vultures / Jim Redmond.
    v. cm. -- (Animals of the rain forest)
Includes bibliographical references (p.   ).
Contents: Range map for King vultures -- King vultures in the rain forest -- What King vultures eat -- A King vulture's life cycle -- The future of King vultures.
  ISBN 0-7398-6837-3 (lib. bdg. : hardcover)
  1. King vulture--Juvenile literature. [1. King vulture. 2. Vultures. 3. Rain forest animals.] I. Title. II. Series.
  QL696.C53 R44 2003
  598.9'2--dc21
                              2002015210
Printed and bound in the United States of America

Produced by Compass Books

Photo Acknowledgments
Tom Stack/Gary Milburn, cover, 6, 18; World Wildlife Fund/Tony Rath, 1, 8, 12, 28-29; Wildlife Conservation Society/D. Demello, 11, 14, 22; Wildlife Conservation Society, 21; Root Resources/Kenneth Fink, 24, 26.

Content Consultants
Dr. Neil Buckley
Biological Sciences Department
State University of New York

Mark Rosenthal
Abra Prentice Wilkin Curator of Large Mammals
Lincoln Park Zoo, Chicago, Illinois

This book supports the National Science Standards.

Some words are shown in bold, **like this**. You can find out what they mean by looking in the Glossary.

Contents

Range Map of King Vultures

MEXICO

BELIZE
HONDURAS
NICARAGUA

GUATEMALA
EL SALVADOR
Caribbean
Sea

COSTA RICA

PANAMA

ECUADOR

COLOMBIA

North
Atlantic
Ocean

VENEZUELA

GUYANA
SURINAME

FRENCH
GUIANA
(FRANCE)

AMAZON
RIVER

PERU

BRAZIL

Range of
King Vultures

Surrounding
Land

Water

Borders

Rivers

BOLIVIA

South
Pacific
Ocean

CHILE

PARAGUAY

South
Atlantic
Ocean

ARGENTINA

URUGUAY

N
W E
S

A Quick Look at King Vultures

What do king vultures look like?

King vulture heads are thinly covered with short, hairlike feathers. The skin on their heads is a mix of colors, such as orange, red, yellow, and purple. They have white bodies with a black band around the edge of their wings. A gray collar of feathers circles their necks.

Where do king vultures live?

King vultures live in wooded lowlands and tropical rain forests from Mexico to Argentina.

What do king vultures eat?

King vultures eat **carrion**. Carrion is the flesh of dead animals.

King vultures are the most colorful kind of vulture.

King Vultures in the Rain Forest

There are 22 kinds of vultures. Like all vultures, the king vulture is a **raptor**. These birds eat mainly meat. All raptors have a strong beak and sharp claws called talons.

The king vulture is one of the largest kinds of vulture. Its wingspan can be up to 6 feet (1.8 meters) long. A wingspan is the distance from the tip of one wing to the tip of the other wing. Its body is about 32 inches (81 centimeters) long and may weigh up to 9 pounds (4.1 kilograms).

The scientific name for king vulture is *Sarcoramphus papa*. The name means "bishop's fleshy beak." King vultures got this name because they have a fold of loose skin above their beaks.

In cold places, king vultures get frostbite. Their toes may fall off, and they will die.

Where do king vultures live?

There are two families of vultures, the New World and the Old World. King vultures are New World vultures. New World vultures live in North and South America. Old World vultures live in Asia, Africa, and Europe. They have things in common with hawks and eagles.

King vultures live mostly in the wooded lowlands and rain forests of South America. They also live in savannas, which are flat grasslands in tropical areas. Their habitat stretches from Argentina all the way up to Mexico. A habitat is a place where an animal or plant usually lives.

A few hundred years ago, king vultures may have lived as far north as Florida. No one knows exactly why they do not live there anymore. Some **ornithologists**, or people who study birds, think that even in Florida the nights are too cold for king vultures. These birds do not do well in cold weather. Frostbite from the cold can hurt their toes. Frostbite happens when body parts are damaged by freezing.

What do king vultures look like?

Like other birds, feathers cover most of a king vulture. Their body feathers are white, but they have black tails. They also have a black band around the edge of their wings. A gray collar of bushy feathers circles their necks.

Unlike most birds, king vulture heads are thinly covered with very short, hairlike feathers. You can see the bright orange, red, yellow, and purple skin covering their head and neck. They also have a loose fold of orange and red skin that sticks out above their nostrils. The skin is called a **wattle**.

A king vulture's beak is thick and red. It is shaped like a hook and ends in a sharp tip. The beak's special shape helps the king vulture rip through thick skin and tear pieces of meat.

King vultures have gray feet. Their long toes bend easily. This helps them grab and hold on to tree branches. Each toe is topped with a heavy, curved claw called a talon.

King vultures have large, white eyes. The eyes are so large that they cannot move them around. To see in different directions, king vultures have to turn their long necks.

This king vulture is using its long toes to hold on to the tree branch.

This king vulture is roosting alone on a perch high in a rain forest tree.

How do king vultures act?

King vultures are solitary birds. Solitary animals mostly live alone instead of in large groups. There is one king vulture in about every 2 square-mile (5.12 square-kilometer) area. King vultures usually fly alone high above the rain forest. Sometimes they fly in pairs.

King vultures are usually dominant. Dominant means most powerful. The king vulture is often the largest vulture at a carcass. All the other kinds of vultures make room for it to eat first. If they did not, the king vulture would fight them.

After eating, king vultures may **roost** with other species of vultures. A species is a group of animals that have some common features. Members of the same species can mate and have young. When vultures roost, they perch somewhere and fall asleep. To perch is to land in a high place and rest. King vultures mainly roost in trees. Sometimes they rest on sandbanks in a river.

King vultures are usually quiet. They do not have a voice box. This means that they cannot whistle or call to each other like other birds do. Instead, king vultures only grunt, cackle, and hiss.

King vultures are scavengers. They usually do not hunt and kill their own food. Instead, they search for and eat food they did not kill.

What Do King Vultures Eat?

King vultures are **carnivores**. Carnivores eat only meat. The main food of king vultures is **carrion**. Carrion is the flesh of dead animals. They may also eat dead fish and small animals.

It is not always easy for a king vulture to find food. Because of this, a king vulture eats as much as it can at one time. It keeps extra food in its **crop**. A crop is a pouch between the throat and stomach that is used to store food.

A king vulture cannot fly when it eats too much food. This puts it in danger from predators. A predator is an animal that eats other animals. If a predator comes too close, the king vulture **regurgitates** its food. Regurgitate means to throw up. When a king vulture regurgitates the heavy food, it becomes lighter. Then it can fly again.

This king vulture is looking for food as it soars through the rain forest.

How do king vultures find food?

Most **raptors** use their excellent eyesight and sense of smell to find food. King vultures may not be able to smell as well as other raptors. They mainly use their eyesight for hunting. To do this, they fly high in the sky. While flying, they look down at the ground. If they see a dead animal, they land and eat it.

King vultures also watch for other circling vultures. Then, they follow these vultures to food. Sometimes it is hard to see dead animals through thick grass and rain forest trees. Observations have shown that king vultures can find bodies that are hidden below the forest canopy.

Some days king vultures fly more than 100 miles (161 kilometers) looking for food. The long, wide shape of their wings helps them **soar**. When a vulture soars, it does not have to flap its wings. Flapping uses a lot of energy. Instead, the king vulture uses jets of warm, rising air called **thermals** to fly. To do this, the king vulture opens its wings. The thermal blows up under the wings and lifts the bird higher into the sky. Soaring helps the vulture save energy because they do not have to flap their wings.

Both male and female king vultures look the same.

A King Vulture's Life Cycle

King vultures mate once a year. What time of year they mate depends on where they live. During this time, they give up their solitary lives. Instead, they try to find another king vulture to mate with and raise young.

To find a mate, a male king vulture performs a dance of struts, bows, and hops for the female. He may repeat this dance five or six times. He also flaps his wings. If the female likes the dance, she becomes his mate.

After mating, king vultures find a place to have their young. They do not build a nest. Instead, they find a tree stump, hollow log, or rock crack. They scratch the place clear of branches and grass to get it ready for having their young.

Young

King vultures lay one white egg, sometimes two. To keep the chick alive and growing, the parents must **incubate** the egg. Incubate means to keep an egg warm. King vulture parents do this by taking turns sitting on the egg.

Raccoons, snakes, and other birds sometimes eat bird eggs. King vultures try to keep their egg safe. They will attack any predator that comes too close.

After 58 days, the chick hatches. Newly hatched chicks are all black. They cannot fly or take care of themselves.

Both the male and female take care of the chick. They feed the chick by **regurgitating** food into its mouth. When the chick grows older, the chick begins to eat more solid food. At four months, the chick is ready to fly.

The color of the chick changes as it grows into an adult bird. After three years, it turns gray. After five years the king vulture becomes an adult, and its feathers turn all white.

Scientists are not sure how long wild king vultures live. King vultures in zoos have lived up to 30 years.

Fluffy white feathers called down cover this chick. Later, it will grow adult flying feathers.

This king vulture is using its beak to clean its body feathers. This is called preening.

A king vulture's day

King vultures are diurnal. This means they are active during the day.

In the morning, a king vulture wakes up and finds a sunny spot. It stretches its wings open. The sun heats the wings and raises its body temperature, which cools down at night.

 A king vulture's mostly bare head helps keep it healthy. If the head had thick feathers, blood and rotting body liquids would soak deep underneath the feathers. A king vulture would not be able to get these feathers clean. Bacteria would grow in the feathers and make the king vulture sick. Because its head has special short, hairlike feathers, blood and bacteria do not stick as much. Its head is easier to keep clean.

Next, the king vulture is ready to eat. It spends hours **soaring** over the trees looking for food. Some days a king vulture does not find any food. Other days, it finds a dead body to eat.

King vultures are messy eaters. After eating, their head is covered with blood and body liquids from the **carrion**. Carrion contains a lot of bacteria. These small living things can make animals sick. After eating, it is important for king vultures to clean themselves to remove any bacteria. Sometimes they take a bath in a river or stream. They also sit in the sun. The sun shines down and kills the bacteria. It also dries the blood and rotted body liquids on its head.

This young king vulture is still mainly black. It will turn white when it is an adult.

The Future of King Vultures

The king vulture is not an **endangered** bird.
Endangered means all of an animal species
may die out in the wild.

The biggest danger to the king vulture is loss
of **habitat**. Habitat is a place where an animal or
plant usually lives. People cut down the rain
forest for wood or to build homes or farms. King
vultures need a lot of space to look for food. As
the rain forest disappears, king vultures have less
space to look for food. There is also less food for
them to find. Without food, king vultures will
starve. Starve means to die from lack of food.

When the rain forests get cut down, king
vultures also lose their homes. They may not be
able to find places to lay their eggs.

▲ King vulture talons and feet are suited for perching, not lifting or carrying.

What will happen to king vultures?

Poison also hurts king vultures. Some farmers in South America use poison to kill coyotes. They do this because they do not want the coyotes to eat their animals. After the coyote dies, the poison stays in its **carcass**. The king vulture then finds and eats the coyote carcass. When it does this, the king vulture eats the poison, too. The poison may not kill the king vulture. But it does make the shells of its eggs thinner. The thin shells are not thick enough to protect the chick. The chick will die before it hatches.

Today, people are learning more about king vultures. Once people killed vultures because they thought the birds were dirty. Now people know that vultures help keep the rain forest clean by eating dead animals.

Some people are trying to save king vultures. If there is not enough food, people sometimes feed king vultures by placing carcasses outside for them to eat. People in Mexico and South America have also passed laws to keep king vultures safe from hunters.

By saving the rain forest, people also help king vultures. Some governments have created wildlife refuges. In these places, it is against the law to hunt or to cut down trees. If the rain forest keeps disappearing, the future of the king vulture is uncertain. But if their rain forests homes are protected, king vultures will live for a long time.

wattle
see page 10

thick beak
see page 10

talons
see page 10

Glossary

carcass—a dead body

carrion—dead and rotting meat

crop—a pouch between the throat and stomach that is used to store food

habitat—a place where an animal or plant usually lives

incubation—keeping eggs warm so they will hatch

ornithologists—people who study birds

raptor—a type of bird that eats meat

regurgitate—to throw up food

roost—to rest or sleep

scavenger—an animal that eats the dead bodies of animals it has not killed

soar—to fly high in the sky without flapping wings

thermal—warm current of rising air

wattle—a loose fold of skin that hangs from the head, neck, or throat of some animals

wingspan—the distance between a bird's wing tips when they are spread

Internet Sites

Belize Zoo: King Vulture
http://www.belizezoo.org/zoo/zoo/birds/vul/
vul1.html

King Vulture
http://www.animalsoftherainforest.com/
kingvulture.htm

Useful Address

Hawk Watch International
P.O. Box 660
Salt Lake City, UT 94110

Books to Read

Rauzon, Mark J. *Vultures*. New York: Franklin
Watts, 1997.

Smith, Roland. *Vultures*. Minneapolis: Lerner
Publications Company, 1997.

Index